Guilty Comfort Foods

Eliza's Secrets

LISA BICK

PHOTOGRAPHY BY TOM CASALINI

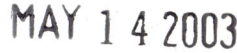

Library of Congress Cataloging-in-Publication Data:
2001118974
Bick, Lisa
Guilty Comfort Foods / by Lisa Bick : photography by Tom Casalini.
ISBN 0-9704410-1-0

Printed in Italy

Sweet Pea Press
10½ North Main Street
Zionsville, Indiana 46077

800-755-3706

Acknowledgments

My thanks and love and credit to:

Tom Casalini, Denise Brunner, Debra Tadevich, Kathy Thalheimer, Susan Kleinman, Robert Stevens, Michael Carlucci, Heather Pinkerton, Debra Weber, Heidi Newman, Jennifer Simmons, Christina Fink

Most of all, my special thanks go to my husband, Stewart, and my children, Hunter, Tenley and Carsten for all of their patience and support, and for eating dessert instead of dinner so frequently.

. . .and a spoonful of jasmine for your soul.

Recipe List

Was she a temptress? Was she an angel?

ONE EGG CAKE

This is one of the recipes written in "grandmother code." It calls for two lumps of butter the size of eggs. She wrote "sweet" milk, which is whole milk (as opposed to sour milk, which is buttermilk). My personal opinion about eggs is that you should use large brown eggs (and make them free range, if you want to be politically correct) because simply by their color, you look like you know what you are doing...and that never hurts. One Egg Cake is blameless with a few fresh berries, or you might purée some fresh or frozen raspberries in your food processor or blender. Toss in a little Grand Marnier and elevate it beyond the farm.

¾ cup sugar

½ cup unsalted butter (softened)

1 egg

1½ cups flour

½ cup whole milk

1½ teaspoons baking powder

½ teaspoon vanilla

½ teaspoon lemon extract

for the topping:

2 tablespoons unsalted butter (softened)

3-4 tablespoons powdered sugar

grated nutmeg

Preheat the oven to 350.

Beat the softened butter and the sugar together until creamy.

Beat in the next six ingredients.

Lightly butter and flour an 8" cake pan, and pour in batter.

Mix softened 2 tablespoons of butter with about 3-4 tablespoons of powdered sugar and a grating of nutmeg and crumble that on top of the cake.

Bake for 25 minutes.

Serving Size: 6

She was the daughter of a farmer, then the wife of a farmer,
but during her greatest moments, perhaps she was only a woman
with a romantic heart.

APPLE DUMPLINGS

It was the apple that tempted Eve, who must have felt that it was far too troublesome to be good all of the time. And let's face it, everyone loves the scintillation of forbidden fruit (or calories) in their mouths. These will make stomachs (and souls) purr with contentment.

2 cups sugar

1 teaspoon ground cinnamon

1 teaspoon ground nutmeg

½ teaspoon unsalted butter

2¼ cups flour

2 teaspoons baking powder

⅔ cup shortening

½ cup whole milk

6 medium apples, peeled and cored

Preheat oven to 375.

For the syrup: Combine 1½ cups of sugar, ½ tsp. cinnamon, ½ tsp. nutmeg and 2½ cups of water. Bring to a boil, reduce the heat and simmer for five minutes. Remove from the heat and stir in the butter. Set aside.

Combine flour, baking powder and ½ tsp. salt in a medium mixing bowl. Cut in the shortening, using a pastry blender or two knives, until the mixture resembles coarse crumbs. Add the milk all at once and stir until moistened. Form into a ball.

On a floured surface, roll the dough out into an 18 x 12 inch rectangle, and then cut it into 6-inch squares. Place an apple in the center of each square. Fill the center of each apple with a mixture of ¾ cup sugar, ½ tsp. cinnamon and ½ tsp. nutmeg. Dot with additional butter.

Moisten the edges of the dough squares and then fold the corners to the center on top of the apples. Pinch the edges together. Place them in a 13 x 9 x 2 inch baking dish. Pour the syrup over the dumplings.

Bake for 45 minutes or until the apples are tender.

Serve them warm with ice cream or cream.

Serving Size: 6

Eliza came of age at the turn of the 20th century,
and I at the turn of the 21st.

COBBLER

This is my favorite. Cobbler sings "Fourth of July." Hope for one of those nights when the heat of the day emanates from the earth and the fireflies rise from the meadows. Dream of having your fill of everything that you desire while you savor every mouthful. Now is not the time to practice moderation. Homemade ice cream on top of it all will make you tremble. Let the fireworks begin!

½ cup butter
1 cup sugar
1 teaspoon salt
1 cup flour
1 teaspoon baking powder
1 cup whole milk
3 cups fresh or frozen fruit

Preheat the oven to 350.

Melt the stick of unsalted butter directly into your baking dish. The size really doesn't matter unless you double this recipe, which will only make you happier.

In a mixing bowl, stir together the sugar, salt, flour and baking powder. Mix in the milk.

Heat the fruit in a saucepan. Add some extra sugar if you would like it even sweeter. (Why not?) You can use any type of berry, and I like to mix fresh peaches and blueberries (*so* Uncle Sam-ish). Plums are also divine, but don't bother peeling them. In a pinch (or in the winter), frozen fruit works, too.

Pour the batter directly into the center of the melted butter. Pour the hot fruit into the center of the batter. Bake for 45 minutes or until it looks golden brown.

I ALWAYS double this recipe. It doesn't matter how many people you serve, there won't be anything left.

"Oh my God!"

Serving Size: 4

TWO-SPICE CAKE

The way this cake smells would make Pavlov himself drool. It's the recipe I will always identify with a sleepy winter afternoon at my grandmother's house. The rich, Christmasy smell woke me and led me, salivating, towards the kitchen. (It's a syrupy memory, but true.) Eat it warm all by itself, or try stirring a little maple syrup into whipped cream and top each warm cake slice with that! This cake is the meaning of the word "cozy." Oh, don't worry; you won't wake up wanting to learn how to crochet.

1 cup unsalted butter (softened)

2¼ cups sugar

5 eggs

3 cups sifted all purpose flour

2 teaspoons ground cloves

½ teaspoon allspice

1 tablespoon cinnamon

1 pinch salt

1 cup buttermilk

1 teaspoon baking soda

Preheat oven to 350 degrees.

Grease a 10" tube pan. In a large mixing bowl and using your electric mixer, cream the butter until it is soft and light. Gradually mix in sugar until the mixture is light and fluffy. In a separate bowl, beat the eggs thoroughly and blend into the creamed mixture.

Sift the flour with the spices and salt and then beat about ⅓ of the flour combination into the batter. Now, stir in ½ of the buttermilk. Add another ⅓ of the flour-spice combination and mix thoroughly. Stir the baking soda into remaining ½ cup of the buttermilk and mix that into the batter along with the remaining flour.

Pour the whole thing into the cake pan and bake for 45-55 minutes, or until the cake tester comes out clean.

Cool ten minutes and turn out onto a cake rack.

Serving Size: 10

While trying to wrap my mind around my own changing dreams,
I tried to find threads of connection to this woman
who came before me.

MA'S DROP SUGAR COOKIES

Sometimes you need comfort for your heart and here is a fine alternative to the usual chocolate chip cookie. Dip them in milk, or coffee if you need the caffeine buzz. Sprinkle with sugar when they come out of the oven. (And, I LOVE the name… Honestly, do you know anyone called "Ma"?)

1 cup sugar

½ cup unsalted butter (softened)

1 egg

2 cups flour

½ cup whole milk

2 teaspoons baking powder

1 teaspoon vanilla

¼ teaspoon nutmeg

¼ teaspoon salt

Preheat the oven to 350 degrees.

Cream together the sugar and butter. Mix in the egg. Sift the flour, baking powder, salt and nutmeg together and add to the creamed mixture, alternating with the milk. Drop by teaspoons onto a greased cookie sheet. Bake for 8-10 minutes.

24 Cookies

The seeds of my imagination romanticized
my grandmother into a slightly exotic woman,
yearning to escape to a different reality.

RAISIN CUSTARD

Even on a "too hot for the mosquitoes" kind of afternoon, this is a simple indulgence. Serve it with cream and eat it under the shade of an old tree and pretend you are Scarlett. Works for me!

2 cups whole milk

½ cup sugar

¾ teaspoon salt

3 tablespoons flour

2 eggs

½ cup raisins

½ teaspoon vanilla extract

Preheat oven to 350.

Heat 1½ cups of milk. Mix together the sugar, salt and flour along with the extra ½ cup of milk. Pour this mix into the hot (not boiling) milk and cook, stirring constantly over low heat until it thickens. Remove from fire (that's what the card says—but just take it off the heat). Beat the eggs in a separate bowl and add them slowly to the hot mixture, whisking the entire time so that the eggs don't scramble. Stir in the raisins and the vanilla. Pour into a buttered baking dish and bake for 30 minutes.

Serving Size: 4

There were very few avenues of opportunity for a young woman
born in southern Indiana in 1884. Like most girls of her time,
she was destined solely to motherhood. By only the age of 36,
she had given birth nine times.

DEPRESSION CAKE

(That's Depression as in historical, not clinical, in case you were wondering.) Lard was the usual shortening used by my grandmother. But honestly, have you ever smelled lard? If you want to be a purist go ahead and use it. I would use butter here, and make sure you stick to the unsalted variety when baking. Another thing to note about this recipe is that you are not limited to raisins. Feel free to use other dried fruit such as apricots or cherries, or even figs. This cake won't depress you unless you think too long about the butter. So, don't.

2 cups sugar

2 cups water

2 cups raisins

1 cup lard
(just kidding! use butter instead)

2 teaspoons ground cloves

2 teaspoons cinnamon

1 teaspoon salt

2 teaspoons baking soda

3 cups flour

2 cups chopped walnuts

Preheat the oven to 325 degrees. Grease and lightly flour a 9 x 4 loaf pan.

Combine the first seven ingredients in a large saucepan and bring to a boil. Boil for a few minutes until it begins to thicken. Cool to lukewarm.

Combine the baking soda, flour and chopped walnuts and stir into the above mixture.

Bake for about one hour or until the tester comes out clean.

Serving Size: 6

Widowed at 38, I believe that her hopes of change slipped into dreams. The mind-numbing hard work of farm life most likely toughened her, but did it break her spirit?

BUTTERMILK BISCUITS

I managed to grab my grandmother's biscuit cutter before the rest of the tribe found it. I love it because I can picture her gnarly hands cutting out hundreds of these at the dreaded family reunions. But you can use a jelly jar, which will make you feel quaint. For a farm breakfast, serve with sausage and gravy, but even I can barely rationalize all of that cholesterol. I use them for strawberry shortcakes. Sprinkle fresh berries with sugar and let them sit all afternoon. Just plop them on top of the warm biscuits and, of course, finish with a generous amount of whipped cream. Try them with soft cream cheese or mascarpone and jam. This recipe is easily doubled.

2 cups all purpose flour

1 tablespoon baking powder

⅓ cup vegetable shortening

**½ teaspoon salt
(or less, depending on your taste)**

1 cup buttermilk

Preheat the oven to 450 degrees.

Toss the first four ingredients into your food processor and then slowly add and blend the buttermilk until a dough ball forms. On a floured board, roll the dough out to about ½ inch thickness and cut out with your jelly jar. Lightly grease an iron skillet or baking pan and nestle them together side by side. Bake for 10 to 15 minutes or until golden brown.

Serving Size: 10

I wonder if she ever wept from exhaustion or loneliness.
I wonder if she tossed and turned at night and rose in the
mornings, resolved to put aside her desires.

CINNAMON ROLLS

Forget the cinnamon rolls in the malls. These are better, and you can add all the butter and sugar that your conscience can handle. (For me, it depends on the day.) Soul food. Enough said.

1 cup whole milk

2 tablespoons sugar

1½ teaspoons salt

¼ cup unsalted butter

2 packages yeast

½ cup warm water

2 eggs (beaten)

5½ cups bread flour

1 cup brown sugar

1 stick (or more) unsalted butter—melted

Scald milk and stir in the sugar, salt and butter. Cool to lukewarm.

Stir yeast into the warm water and set aside.

Pour the milk and yeast mixtures into a large bowl. Add eggs and 2 cups of flour and beat with a wooden spoon. Stir in enough of the remaining flour to make a soft dough. Turn out onto a lightly floured board or counter top and knead until smooth and elastic, about 8-10 minutes. (If you don't want to burn calories and improve your biceps, use the dough blade in your food processor or dough hook with a heavy duty mixer.) Oil a large bowl and place the dough in it—turning to coat the dough with the oil. Cover the bowl with a warm, wet cloth and let it rise in a warm place until doubled in bulk, about one hour.

Punch down and turn it out onto a lightly floured board. Divide the dough into three equal parts. Roll the first piece into a rectangle about 14 x 9 inches. Brush lightly with the melted butter (a lot, ok?). Crumble the brown sugar over the top (about one cup). Sprinkle with cinnamon. Beginning with the short edge, roll up the rectangle while slightly stretching out the roll. Seal the edge by pinching. Now, slice into 1-inch-thick rolls and place them side by side in a buttered baking dish. Let the rolls rise until doubled in bulk. Do the same thing with the other two parts.

Bake until golden (30 minutes), 375 degree oven.

Serving Size: 10

CREAM PIES—COCONUT, BANANA OR CHOCOLATE

This is original sin. Make these when you want to be very bad. But hey! They have dairy, protein, fruit, and carbs and are high in calcium, proving that even wickedness can be good for you. Trust me, neither cowboys nor angels, nor sailors nor saints can say no to cream anything.

½ cup sugar

4 tablespoons flour

2 cups milk

1 teaspoon vanilla

2 cups whole milk

1 cup shredded coconut

You will need a pre-baked 9" pie shell for this pie. I obviously would like you to make the pie crust in this book, but use your own, or even buy a frozen one if you must. I just want you to know that your grandmother would scoff. Mix together the sugar and flour. Add milk, slowly at first, then all at once. Cook mixture in medium sauce pan over medium heat, stirring constantly until scalded. Beat the yolks and temper them by adding ⅓ of the cooked mixture to them, beating quickly. Add the egg mixture to the rest of the cooked mixture and while whisking constantly, cook until thick. Remove from heat. Add vanilla. Pour into bowl over ice bath and cool, stirring occasionally.

meringue:

2 large egg whites

dash salt

¼ cup sugar

For the meringue, beat the whites until frothy. Add a pinch of salt and beat until soft peaks form. Slowly add the sugar while beating until stiff peaks form. Pour the filling into the pre-baked pie shell and top with meringue, sealing edges. Brown the meringue in a 350 degree oven with the door open. Watch carefully! Chill at least two hours and preferably overnight.

If you are making a Coconut pie, mix ¾ cup of the coconut into the filling and sprinkle the other ¼ cup over the top of the meringue. If you want Banana Cream, slice a layer of bananas into the pie shell. Add filling and another layer of bananas, then top with the meringue. If you want Chocolate, mix 4 tablespoons of dutch cocoa into the sugar and flour mixture and proceed with or without the meringue.

Remember that if you eat all of the custard directly from the bowl, there won't be a pie for anyone else.

Serving Size: 8

She must have faced days when her eyes searched
the mirror for the woman she was before the neediness
of nine children became her mantra.

PIE CRUST

If you are feeling like you should be on the Continent instead of in your kitchen, just roll out the dough into a rough circle, lay it on a cookie sheet, fill it with a mixture of fruit and sugar and a dash of cinnamon. Voilà! French country tart. (Sounds risqué!) Want to hide the extra dough? Cut the excess into little squares and sprinkle with sugar and cinnamon, and bake them alone as little treats just for you. You can worry about it for about five minutes if you must.

4 cups all purpose flour

1¾ cups vegetable shortening

1 tablespoon sugar

2 teaspoons salt

1 tablespoon apple cider vinegar

1 egg

½ cup cold water

Combine the flour, shortening, sugar and salt. Honestly, I use the food processor and pulse this together. In a separate bowl, beat the egg with a fork and add the vinegar and water. Toss that into the processor and pulse together just until it is combined. Do not over beat this. Press the dough into a ball in your hands. Chill in the fridge for at least 15 minutes, or refrigerate for up to three days. Roll it out on a floured board (a slab of marble is great, of course).

This makes two, nine-inch double crusts (top and bottom) or four singles. Be sure to vent the top crust. Carve your initials if you're feeling narcissistic.

Stitching crazy quilts spangled with stars as a means
of comfort and warmth for her children surely enlisted her heart and
her hands, but were there moments when she longed to be stitching a
red silk dress for herself instead?

WACKY CAKE

One-pan chocolate guilt

1½ cups sifted all purpose flour

1 cup sugar

1 teaspoon baking soda

3 tablespoons cocoa

¼ teaspoon salt

1 teaspoon vanilla

6 tablespoons safflower oil
(or corn oil, or vegetable oil)

1 tablespoon apple cider vinegar

1 cup cold water

Preheat oven to 350.

Using an ungreased 9 x 9 inch baking pan, sift the first 5 ingredients together directly into the pan. Make a hole in the center and add the next 4 ingredients (the wet ones!).

Stir gently until thoroughly moistened. Bake 20-25 minutes until a sharp knife stuck into the center comes out clean. Dust with confectioners' sugar or serve with ice cream or whipped cream…depending on how much guilt you can handle.

This is the absolute easiest!

Serving Size: 1 or more

Did she ever have one night of romance? And, if so, did her head take her home to her responsibilities—or did her heart win that dance? Were there shining moments only for herself?

BLUEBERRY CAKE

You know, there are countless restaurants serving exotic fare like pan-roasted Chilean sea bass with artichoke ravioli and Barigoule vinaigrette, but would someone please just serve Blueberry Cake? Straightforward, easy, delectable and uncomplicated gets my attention. This beats the muffin routine, so serve it for breakfast. After a five-star dinner, your body will thank you.

½ cup unsalted butter

1 cup sugar

2 eggs

1⅔ cups flour

2 teaspoons baking powder

¼ teaspoon salt

½ teaspoon cinnamon

½ cup milk—preferably whole

1½ cups fresh blueberries

Preheat oven to 350.

Grease and flour an 8 x 8 x 2 iron skillet. If you don't have one, you should, but you could use a cake pan of the same size if you want.

Cream together the sugar and the butter. Add the eggs and beat to blend. Sift the flour, the baking powder, the salt, and the cinnamon together and alternately add the dry ingredients and the milk into the creamed butter mixture. Gently fold in the fresh blueberries. Pour into skillet or cake pan.

Bake for 55 minutes or until the center springs back from your touch. Dust with confectioners' sugar.

Serving Size: 6

I don't know the answers. I am only the recipient of her small gifts. The thinning quilts, well loved, and the scrawled recipes of sweet abandon are now mine.

COCONUT CAKE

This is one of the few recipes that cannot be whipped together on a whim. The cake has to cool, and of course you have to find the perfect cake plate for dramatic effect. Be sure to spread some icing between the layers. This is pretty and luscious and because I love coconut, it's an act of self-indulgence just in creating it. Not only that, but you could take it to the state fair and win based on the way it looks, which is fairly racy, if you ask me.

½ cup unsalted butter (softened)

1½ cups sugar

3 eggs

1½ teaspoons vanilla

1¼ cups buttermilk

1¼ cups shredded coconut

2¼ cups flour

1½ teaspoons baking powder

1 teaspoon salt

½ teaspoon baking soda

icing:

½ cup sugar

½ cup white corn syrup

2 tablespoons water

¼ cup egg whites

1 teaspoon vanilla

Preheat oven to 375.

Cream together the butter and the sugar. Beat the eggs and the vanilla together with a fork and slowly add to the butter mixture. Combine the buttermilk with 1 cup of coconut. Combine the flour, baking powder, salt and baking soda and add alternately with the buttermilk to the batter.

Grease and flour two 8" or 9" cake pans. Pour the batter into the pans.

Bake for 25-30 minutes. Cool on cake racks.

For the icing: In a saucepan, blend the sugar, syrup and water. Bring to a rapid boil.

Beat the egg whites until stiff peaks form. Pour the hot syrup into the egg whites, beating constantly until it once again comes to stiff peaks. Blend in the vanilla. Ice the cake and sprinkle with remaining coconut.

Serving Size: 8

DEEP DISH APPLE PIE

*Fruit for breakfast? Why not make it memorable? Serve it warm
in the morning and the cereal crowd will love you for all eternity.*

10-12 tart cooking apples

½ cup sugar

2 tablespoons fresh lemon juice

1 cup flour

½ cup brown sugar, packed

½ cup unsalted butter (one stick!)

Preheat oven to 375.

Pare and core the apples and chop them into small pieces.

Combine in medium bowl with the sugar and lemon juice. Spoon into a buttered 9" shallow baking dish. In a separate bowl, combine the flour and the brown sugar and cut in the butter with a pastry blender or two knives. Sprinkle over the apples and pat down with your fingers.

Bake 45 minutes or until the juice bubbles around the edge and the top is golden brown.

Serving Size: 6

It is conceivable that in the corners of her days, she was both an angel and a temptress; pounding the sensual bread dough into warm treats while kneading the fires of her soul.

CHOCOLATE ROLL

Sometimes it is invigorating to tiptoe on the edge of a volcano. Chocolate can also be dangerous or invigorating, but when the blast of pleasure-inducing endorphins kicks in, everyone is happy. This is bliss.

5 eggs

1 cup sugar

6 ounces dark sweet chocolate

3 tablespoons cold water

⅛ cup cocoa

1 cup cream

½ teaspoon vanilla

Preheat oven to 350 degrees.

Separate eggs. Butter a jelly roll sheet, and cover it with wax paper, then butter again. Beat ¾ cup sugar into egg yolks, to a creamy consistency. Break up chocolate into a saucepan and add 3 tablespoons of cold water. Melt slowly on lowest setting (or use a double boiler). Cool and add slowly to the egg yolk mixture.

Beat the egg whites until stiff peaks form. Stir them into the chocolate mixture. Mix gently, but thoroughly.

Spread evenly on the baking sheet. Bake 10 minutes at 350 and 5 minutes more at 275-300. Remove from the oven.

Cover the top with a cloth soaked in cold water and wrung out. Cool and refrigerate for 1 hour. Carefully remove from the pan with a spatula. Dust with cocoa.

Turn over on wax paper and very carefully peel off the paper from the top.

Whip the cream with the remaining ¼ cup sugar and add vanilla. Spread the cream over the entire surface and roll it up like a jelly roll.

Serving Size: 8

In the bottom of the stairwell closet at my grandmother's house,

I was the one who found the faded pink box.

SUGAR CREAM PIE

This is the basic grandmother pie. Simple and sweet and not at all as rich as you would expect when scanning the ingredients. Try skipping the pie crust and make a fruit compote by gently heating some fresh blueberries with a handful of sugar and pouring the baked filling over the berries. You could also bake the whole thing and toss some fresh berries of any sort on top.

Be sure to use a 9" pie shell or older pie tin or you will have to double the recipe to fill the lovely new French ceramic pie dishes. That tells me that maybe it is just the modern portions that are outrageous, not these great desserts.

1 cup sugar

½ cup flour

1 teaspoon salt

1 pint heavy cream

2 tablespoons butter

½ teaspoon cinnamon

You will need an unbaked pie shell before you even start.

Preheat oven to 425 degrees.

In a mixing bowl, stir together the flour, sugar and salt. Stir in the cream.

Pour mixture into the unbaked pie shell. Dot with shaved butter and sprinkle with cinnamon.

Bake at 425 for 25 minutes and then turn the oven down to 375 and bake another 30 minutes.

Serving Size: 6

When I opened the door, the familiar pungent, rosewater pastry scent that only a grandmother's house emits made me catch my breath with the thrill of discovery.

COTTAGE PUDDING

Don't bargain with your abs of steel mentality over this recipe.
I think it is low on the self-blame scale—and it even sounds like a grandmother is spoiling you.

2 eggs

1 cup sugar

2 tablespoons unsalted butter

½ cup whole milk

1 teaspoon baking powder

1½ cups flour

sauce:

1½ cups boiling water

1 cup sugar

2 tablespoons unsalted butter

flour

Preheat the oven to 350 degrees.

Cream together the butter and the sugar. Add the eggs and beat until light. Sift the flour and baking powder together and add, alternating with the milk, to the batter. Pour this batter into a 9 x 9 inch cake pan or iron skillet that you have greased lightly. Mix together the boiling water, the cup of sugar and the 2 tablespoons of butter. Whisk in enough flour to make it about the consistency of gravy. Pour this over the top of the batter and bake for 40 minutes—or until golden brown on the top.

It's a surprise when the "sauce" that you pour over the top sinks to the bottom and the cake batter rises. Serve it warm (to keep the sauce soft) and top it with some strawberries and sugar or melted red currant jam.

Serving Size: 6

A copper washtub full of old photos and loose patchwork pieces
yielded the box. Inside were handwritten recipes on
slips of yellowed paper, intermingled with a few letters of little
consequence, detailing her daily duties.

BLACKBERRY PUDDING

My cousin and I had to go out into the blackberry patch and pick blackberries for my grandmother. A nasty job, full of thorns and mosquitoes, and worst of all, chiggers. Thousands of them. She promised us that the pudding would be worth it and it was—even though our legs were painted with spots of red nail polish to stop the bites from itching. (Don't ask.) Now that you are a grown-up, stay out of the blackberry patch, because it ruins a manicure. This is not a romantic dessert, but it's just so full of summer solstice it makes you want to dance.

3 eggs
2 cups whole milk
4 cups flour
5 teaspoons baking powder
3 cups blackberries

for the sauce:
2 tablespoons unsalted butter
1 cup sugar
whipping cream
juice of 1 lemon
pinch of ground nutmeg

Preheat oven to 350.

Beat the eggs until light in color and stir in the milk. Sift the flour with the baking powder and beat gradually into the egg mixture. Dredge the blackberries in a little extra flour and stir them into the batter. Pour into a greased baking dish. Bake, covered, for an hour. Uncover and brown just a bit.

Serve with a hard sauce made by whisking together the butter (softened), one cup of sugar and enough whipping cream to make a thick sauce. Beat in the juice of one lemon and a pinch of nutmeg. Spoon on top of the pudding.

Serving Size: 6

BRITTLE

You need a slab of marble for this. It looks good in your kitchen and makes YOU look like a professional. Besides, you really do need it for rolling out pastry doughs. If you are using peanuts in this brittle, use raw peanuts because they will cook during the process. If you are using pecans (sexier, but don't take my advice), only raise the heat to 290 and watch it or they will burn. And, if you are allergic to nuts…don't use any. This is great without them, too. When you add the baking soda, it will foam like a science experiment, so it is imperative that you stir it vigorously at this point. Use a very large pan to compensate for all of this foaming action. Cut the recipe in half if you haven't been to the gym this week. Double it if you have.

5 cups sugar

1 pound nuts (raw, if using peanuts)

1 cup corn syrup

½ cup unsalted butter

4 teaspoons baking soda

1 teaspoon salt

1 cup hot water

In a large saucepan, stir together the sugar, salt and hot water. Heat to 250 degrees (you will need a candy thermometer for this one). Add peanuts and heat to 295 degrees. If you are using pecans, heat only to 290. Add the butter, stirring until melted. Remove from heat and add baking soda. Stir vigorously and pour onto previously buttered slab of marble. Starting at the periphery of the molten mass, pull the edges to stretch the brittle until 4 x 6 inch pieces can be separated from the center. Lay the pieces aside on wax paper or the shiny side of freezer paper, or on another piece of marble. The stretching is very important as this makes very thin and very tender brittle that will NOT break your teeth…(not a good thing).

Serving Size: 4

The excitement came with the cobalt silk ribbon that loosely tied the bundle together. Was it a ribbon from her childhood brunette waves or was it a treasure from a long lost love?

RHUBARB CHARLOTTE

I am going to give this one up to you. Just read the directions and try it on your own. It's delicious, if you are into rhubarb. I like it, but I go heavy on the sugar.

white bread crumbs

fresh rhubarb

sugar

unsalted butter

nutmeg

Butter a baking dish and cover the bottom an inch deep with fine bread crumbs. Over this, place a layer of rhubarb that has been cut into short lengths. Cover with sugar, then add another layer of crumbs and dot with bits of butter. Keep alternating the crumbs and fruit until the dish is full, saving crumbs for the top. Sprinkle nutmeg over the top and bake for an hour or until browned.

Serving Size: 6

Somehow, this box said as much as any journal from the past
millennium. Eliza seemed to be saying, "Here are my dreams,
my joy, and my fears. Here is my womanhood." Unraveling
her mysteries begins and ends with this tied package.

DOUGHNUTS

Does anything say "bad for you" like a doughnut? Probably not. So that is all the more reason to show how strong you can be by only eating one. These are really indulgent and worth the effort…which is substantial. Nothing good comes easily—just ask your therapist, who you will probably have to see tomorrow, because you WON'T be able to eat just one (self-control issue). The recipe says to cut out the doughnuts with a biscuit cutter (use a jelly jar) and make a hole in the center with a large thimble. You don't own a thimble? Try a small aspirin (or sleeping pill!) bottle. Eat them warm and swoon.

1 cup sugar

3½ teaspoons baking powder

½ teaspoon cinnamon

½ teaspoon nutmeg

½ teaspoon salt

4 cups all purpose flour

2 eggs

1 cup whole milk

3 tablespoons unsalted butter, melted

vegetable shortening
melted to 1" depth in pan

Sift together the sugar, baking powder, cinnamon, nutmeg, salt and flour. Beat the eggs thoroughly, then stir them into the dry ingredients. Add the milk and melted butter and beat until the dough comes together. On a floured board, roll the dough out to about ⅓ inch in thickness and cut with a jelly jar. Make the holes with a thimble or pill bottle. Heat the shortening in a generous pan to 375 degrees. You will need a deep fat thermometer for this. When a 1-inch bread cube browns in 60 seconds, it is ready. Fry several doughnuts at a time until they are golden. Drain on paper towels. Dust with sugar or powdered sugar.

Nostalgia is a funny thing. It can make you regret

all that you have not done and nothing that you have.

BAKED PEACH PUDDING

*Warm peaches in any form are delectable and sensuous. Under summer stars,
what could be more comforting than this pudding with a scoop of vanilla or even hazelnut ice cream?
Well, a few things, but it's all about attitude.*

3 cups fresh peaches

¾ cup sugar

½ cup milk

4 tablespoons unsalted butter

½ teaspoon salt

1 teaspoon baking powder

1 teaspoon vanilla extract

1 cup flour

topping:

1 cup sugar

1 tablespoon cornstarch

¼ teaspoon salt

Preheat oven to 325 degrees.

Peel and slice the peaches. Here is a trick that my grandmother used: She would make an X slice on the bottom of the peaches with a sharp knife, just slicing the skin. Then she would drop the whole peaches into boiling water until the scored skin began to curl. Run them under cool water and the peels should slip off.

Butter an 8 x 8 inch baking pan or ceramic dish (or the iron skillet) and layer the peaches onto the bottom. Pour the batter over the top of the peaches. Sift the topping of the sugar, cornstarch and salt over the top of the batter.

Pour one cup of boiling water over the entire thing and bake for 50 minutes.

Serving Size: 8

Remembrances melt with time, but these recipes
evoked sugared memories of her, as well as my own desire
to create tender nostalgia for those I love.

RICE PUDDING

This is perfect for sick kids and lonely hearts. Plus, it is a great way to use all the extra rice that comes with Chinese carry-out. Rich and sweet, the rice nevertheless falls into the "grains" food group, so serve it for breakfast (or any meal, for that matter). A little cream poured over the top and a dash of cinnamon complete the warm and cozy scenario. You can curl into the deep sofa cushions and mumble, "Let them eat pudding."

2 cups sweet milk (whole milk)

1 cup cold cooked white rice

¾ cup sugar

1 teaspoon vanilla

¼ teaspoon salt

2 eggs

cinnamon (optional)

This is microwavable—and so fast that way. Beat the eggs, separately, before stirring everything together in a micro-safe bowl. Bake on high for about 3 minutes. Stir it and bake another 5-7 minutes, watching carefully because all microwaves vary. When it reaches the pudding texture you like, take it out and stir it once before serving.

Serving Size: 3

Rich histories can be made in the kitchen—among other places.
The kitchen was a place of indulgence for my grandmother
and for me. While tossing together combinations of butter, sugar
and eggs, it is easy to let the imagination soar.

FLOATING ISLAND

The possibilities are endless: Take me away to an island. No man is an island. Treasure Island. Floating Island? It is uncomplicated, and the rose flower water will remind you of faded cabbage rose wallpaper and lace curtains, even if all of those eggs only remind you of cholesterol. Send in the moist twilight of a June evening in the hills of southern Indiana and at least pretend you are floating on an island. (A margarita would maybe help a little bit, too.)

1 quart whole milk

6 eggs (large)

2 tablespoons sugar

1 teaspoon rose water

(or lemon or vanilla extract)

coconut or sugar for topping

Separate the eggs. Set aside the whites. Beat the yolks with a whisk or fork until blended together. Now, beat the whites to soft peaks.

Bring the milk to almost boiling and stir in the yolks, beating quickly the entire time. Beat in the sugar, and stir constantly until it thickens, being careful not boil. When it reaches pudding consistency, pour it into a shallow dish.

Pour the whites over the hot custard and the whites will cook slightly. Chill. Sprinkle with coconut or a little sugar and serve cold.

Serving Size: 6

*I think there were sultry afternoons when the pies came out of
the oven that she sat down at the scrubbed raw table and soothed
her hungers with creamy custard. She deserved it. Her life left
no room for guilt about anything, especially good food.*

SHOO-FLY PIE

This has a full-flavored cake texture. I have to admit that this is the one recipe that scared me, but I am surprised by its comfort on a blustery autumn or winter night. I love it with baked apples or vanilla ice cream and coffee. Of course, I love anything with ice cream, but this is really unusual and filling. Perhaps some mulled apple cider would sell it to everyone else. You can simply top it with confectioners' sugar or even, of course!, whipped cream. "Shoo-fly, don't bother me…"

1 unbaked pie shell

2 cups flour

1 cup sugar

8 tablespoons unsalted butter, melted

½ cup sorghum syrup
(I use robust flavored molasses)

1 teaspoon baking soda

1 cup hot water

Preheat the oven to 450.

Use old-sized pie tins or Pyrex pie plates that are 9½ inches in diameter. I decided that you need a whole stick of butter, but don't tell anyone. Crumb together the flour, sugar and melted butter and place it into the bottom of an unbaked pie shell. (Homemade is best, but cheat if you want.) Stir water and baking soda into the molasses and pour over the first layer in the pie crust. Mix together with your fingers! (OK, it's gross, but worth it.)

Bake for 15 minutes at 450 degrees, then 25 more at 350. When it springs back from the touch at the center it is done.

Serving Size: 8

This is my tribute to a woman whose scattered secrets were
left for me along with her recipes of comfort. They have taught me
that it takes a brave woman to perform a balancing act
in the center ring of unreasonable obstacles.

OATMEAL CAKE

By virtue of having been raised Catholic, I harbor guilt about everything. The health benefits of fiber are very real, so I drop the guilt while eating half of this all by myself. It's good for me! It is sticky and sweet and I love it absolutely plain. I eat it with a silver spoon.

½ cup boiling water
1 cup oatmeal (not quick)
½ cup unsalted butter
1 cup brown sugar
1 cup white sugar
2 beaten eggs
1½ cups flour
1 teaspoon cinnamon
1 teaspoon baking soda
¼ teaspoon salt

topping:
6 tablespoons butter
¼ cup cream
1 cup brown sugar
½ teaspoon vanilla
1 cup shredded coconut

Preheat the oven to 350.

Bring the butter to room temperature. Boil the water and add the oats. Remove from heat and let cool for about 20 minutes. Cream the butter and add the sugars, beating together. Beat the 2 eggs separately, and add to the butter mixture. Stir in the oatmeal.

Sift together the flour, cinnamon, baking soda, and salt and stir it into the batter.

Grease and flour a 9" square cake pan. Pour the cake ingredients into the pan. Bake for 30 minutes. Now you can make the topping by simply beating together the 6 tablespoons of butter with the cream, brown sugar and vanilla. Stir in the coconut. Spread mixture on the cake and return to the oven for 10 minutes more.

Serving Size: 8

CHEWY DATE DESSERT

*"Butter the size of a walnut" is what the recipe says, but my unit of measurement is a golf ball,
so I would say 3-4 tablespoons, but who's counting? This also calls for rolled breadcrumbs. My grandmother
always made her own potato bread and when stale, she squashed it under her formidable rolling pin.
You may use any good white bread that you have left out on the counter overnight and chop it in your
food processor. Rolled oats = oatmeal. Any nut will do for this, but I really love hazelnuts.
Texture is stimulating. This recipe liberates the date in my mind.*

1 cup sugar

1 cup chopped dates

½ cup nuts

1 cup rolled oats (oatmeal)

1 cup rolled bread crumbs

1 egg

1 cup whole milk

1 teaspoon baking powder

1 lump unsalted butter the size of
a walnut, melted

whipped cream to top

Preheat the oven to…the paper says a "slow" oven. I take that to mean about 325 degrees.

Grease an 8 x 8 pan. Combine the bread crumbs and the baking powder in the food processor. Beat in the egg. Add the sugar and milk to the bread crumb mixture. Stir in the oats, nuts, chopped dates and the melted butter. Bake for 30 minutes. Serve with whipped cream, which you can put on just about anything that you serve.

Serving Size: 6